Approaching CHRISTMAS

To my Mother, with love

Approaching CHRISTMAS

JANE WILLIAMS

LION

Published by Lion Books
an imprint of
Lion Hudson plc
Wilkinson House, Jordan Hill Road,
Oxford OX2 8DR, England
www.lionhudson.com/lion
ISBN 978 0 7459 5590 2

First edition 2005
This edition 2012

A catalogue record for this book is available from the British Library

Printed and bound in China, July 2012, LH17

Contents

Preface

I love Christmas. I love everything about it. I love standing in supermarket queues, where everyone is queueing for things they wouldn't normally dream of buying, and I love exchanging wry smiles with other parents in toy shops. I love the carols we sing in church in Advent, the four weeks of waiting before Christmas, and I love Christmas carols, too. I love the fact that Christmas is enjoyed all over the world, and that everyone thinks that there is only one way to celebrate Christmas, only all those ways are different. I've experienced Christmas in India, England, Wales and America and each was different but perfect.

As I shop and walk and drive around at Christmas, I'm always struck by the festive atmosphere. People seem to know that Christmas is a time for joy, even if they couldn't quite say why. It's as though there is a deep instinct in us that Christmas is a time for seeing the good in each other and the world. As a Christian, I want to share my reasons for believing that that instinct is sound, but I also want to learn from the joy around me. In the meditations that follow, I am trying to make connections between the joys of celebrating Christmas that we share and the spiritual meaning that we might see in the way we decorate our houses or give gifts at Christmas time. My hope is that readers who already have a faith might find these ideas illuminating, and that readers who simply want to bring more reverence and depth to the celebration of Christmas might find some of the ideas and pictures helpful for meditating on life at this time. Like most religious writing and speaking, these thoughts are primarily aimed at the author. The deeper reality of Christmas can so easily be swallowed up by its sheer busyness. But, on the other hand, I want to be able to go on seeing Christmas as fun, as well as meaningful.

At Christmas we celebrate gift and generosity and open expressions of love. You don't need religion to understand that all of those things make life worth living. The Christian story suggests that gift and generosity and love are basic to what God does at Christmas, but also that religious people sometimes need to relearn this truth from others who have the Christmas spirit, even if they don't know the Christmas story.

If I know anything about Christmas, I learned it from my mother, who will always symbolize the spirit of Christmas for me. Every year she produced warmth and presents and love for a large family from small resources, and made us feel that the world was a place of generosity and trust. I dedicate this book to her, with love.

*I*n those days a decree went out from Emperor Augustus that all the world should be registered. This was the first registration and was taken while Quirinius was governor of Syria. All went to their own towns to be registered. Joseph also went from the town of Nazareth in Galilee to Judea, to the city of David called Bethlehem, because he was descended from the house and family of David. He went to be registered with Mary, to whom he was engaged and who was expecting a child. While they were there, the time came for her to deliver her child. And she gave birth to her firstborn son and wrapped him in bands of cloth, and laid him in a manger, because there was no place for them in the inn.

In that region there were shepherds living in the fields, keeping watch over their flock by night. Then an angel of the Lord stood before them, and the glory of the Lord shone around them, and they were terrified. But the angel said to them, 'Do not be afraid; for see – I am bringing you good news of great joy for all the people: to you is born this day in the city of David a Saviour, who is the Messiah, the Lord. This will be a sign for you: you will find a child wrapped in bands of cloth and lying in a manger. And suddenly there was with the angel a multitude of the heavenly host, praising God and saying,

'Glory to God in the highest heaven, and on earth peace among those whom he favours!'

When the angels had left them and gone into heaven, the shepherds said to one another, 'Let us now go to Bethlehem and see this thing that has taken place, which the Lord has made known to us.' So they went with haste and found Mary and Joseph, and the child lying in the manger. When they saw this, they made known what had been told them about this child; and all who heard it were amazed at what the shepherds told them. But Mary treasured all these words and pondered them in her heart. The shepherds returned, glorifying and praising God for all they had heard and seen, as it had been told them.

LUKE 2:1–20

CHAPTER 1

Christmas Spirit

The weeks before Christmas tend to be very busy in our house nowadays. We have lots of parties and carol services for all the different people who help an Archbishop of Canterbury to do his job, and we also have school concerts and plays to fit in, while trying still to get some ordinary work done. Rushing from one engagement to the next can begin to seem like an end in itself, to the point where I almost forget why it is that we're doing all these things in the first place. The word 'Christmas' may appear in the title of all the invitations, but there really isn't time to think about Christmas itself, because I'm just too busy. I find myself getting nostalgic for childhood days, when the excitement of Christmas built up slowly over the last few weeks of term, and all I had to do was look forward to it. I suspect my parents viewed the matter slightly differently, and were as overworked as I now feel, but if so, they kindly concealed it from us children. When I found myself seriously considering having salad for Christmas dinner this year, I realized that drastic measures were necessary. I needed to rediscover Christmas.

It seemed like a good idea to go back and read about the first Christmas and the birth of the baby Jesus. I imagine that Jesus' mother, Mary, remembered how she first discovered that she was going to have a baby. It would have been hard to forget, as an angel came to announce it to her! Mary was clearly a remarkable person. The only question she asks the angel is about the mechanics – how is she, a virgin, to get pregnant? As soon as the angel has answered that, Mary says, 'OK'. She is fiercely glad that God has asked her to do this thing, but although she is rightly proud of her own role, she also knows that this is not just about her. The Bible shows that it is about God coming to establish a new world order, and to be close to the poor and the powerless. Part of Mary's memory is suddenly seeing what God was doing and being filled with a joy that made her sing aloud.

My soul magnifies the Lord, and my spirit rejoices in God my Saviour, for he has looked with favour on the lowliness of his servant. Surely, from now on all generations shall call me blessed; for the Mighty One has done great things for me, and holy is his name. His mercy is for those who fear him from generation to generation. He has shown strength

with his arm; he has scattered the proud in the thoughts of their hearts. He has brought down the powerful from their thrones and lifted up the lowly; he has filled the hungry with good things, and sent the rich away empty.

LUKE 1:46–53

Then Mary remembers the long, hard journey she had to make, just before the baby was born. She and her husband Joseph had to travel from Nazareth to Bethlehem to take part in a national census, and the regulations don't make any allowances for heavily pregnant women.

So Mary remembers the jolting movements of the donkey that carried her, and the weight of the baby inside her as she walked. And, of course, she remembers what it was like to give birth to her first child in a stable, with none of her family there to help her, only Joseph and a few kind strangers. Then she remembers the odd visitors who came to see the new baby. First some shepherds, who said a host of angels had sent them, and then, much later, some foreigners, who said that they had been led to her baby by a star. Mary remembers wondering what on earth she had let herself in for by saying yes to God's angel all those months ago. She remembers thinking about the shepherds and the wise men and wondering just what it was going to be like to bring up a baby whose birth was surrounded by such strange events.

Joseph's memories of the birth of their baby start with an angel, too, just like Mary's. It may even be the same angel. Who knows? This one comes to Joseph in a dream and tells him that his fiancée, Mary, is going to have a baby. Joseph knows it isn't his, but the angel assures him that Mary is to be trusted, and that he must marry her as planned and take care of her and the baby. Joseph remembers shouldering that weight of responsibility, knowing that it must be important if God's angel says so. Joseph remembers all the planning he had to do, to get Mary safely to Bethlehem and take care of her while the baby was born. He knows he didn't make a brilliant job of it – it would have been

better if he could have found a comfortable hotel for Mary to stay in — but he did his best. Like Mary, he remembers the odd visitors. They were only really interested in the baby, and Joseph remembers feeling left out and a bit anxious. Quite rightly, as it turns out, because the foreigners who have come following some star have stupidly alerted King Herod to the birth of the baby, and Herod wants to get rid of him, in case he turns out to be a challenge to Herod's power. So Joseph remembers having to pack up and take the family away to Egypt in the middle of the night.

It wasn't the easiest thing to arrange, but he had promised the angel, and anyway he had begun to love the new baby too, so it wasn't just a matter of duty anymore.

It is fascinating to have these two different insights into the events of the first Christmas. But if Mary and Joseph's memories highlight different things as important, they do have some common themes. Most significant of all is their insight into the way God acts. It seems that the world looks very different through God's eyes and through ours. We may overestimate what we have to do to please God. Mary and Joseph only had to say yes, and God was pleased that they were willing to be part of the divine plan. Kings and rulers, bankers and priests like the world-order the way it is, and distrust this mad streak in God. They are not the ones that the angels visit. Mary and Joseph are excited simply to be working with God, and they don't care about what they are going to get out of it for themselves.

This, I believe, is at heart the spirit of Christmas. It is a willingness to value something else above our own personal comfort and security. It is a wild delight in other people, however inconvenient they might be. It is like Mary's willingness to have the baby who is going to cause her so much grief, and Joseph's determination to protect them both, even though the child isn't his. It is like God's desire to come and live with creation, even though it will not recognize God as its maker. That's why, I think, the Christmas spirit is best symbolized by presents, by giving things away, just for the fun of it.

In Charles Dickens's book *A Christmas Carol*, Scrooge's young nephew puts this into words:

> *'But I am sure I have always thought of Christmas time, when it has come round – apart from the veneration due to its sacred name and origin, if anything belonging to it can be apart from that – as a good time: a kind, forgiving, charitable, pleasant time: the only time I know of, in the long calendar of the year, when men and women seem by one consent to open their shut-up hearts freely, and to think of people below them as if they really were fellow-passengers to the grave, and not another race of creatures bound on other journeys. And therefore, uncle, though it has never put a scrap of gold or silver in my pocket, I believe that it* has *done me good, and* will *do me good; and I say, God bless it!'*

Scrooge's nephew doesn't expect this open-heartedness to last all year, but he still feels that it is, in some undefined kind of way, 'good'. Even those who are more bitter, or cynical, or just plain realistic, join in the attempt to preserve the illusions of Christmas. They may not believe that Christmas will make any difference to us grown-ups, but they connive at a fantasy world for children. Children, at least, must be allowed to go on believing in the 'Christmas spirit' for a few years before they have to face the grim reality of the world. But whether the cynics

would admit it or not, their attitude, just as much as that of the optimist, reveals an instinctive longing for a magical solution to things and a yearning for a 'happy ever after' world. 'They lived happily ever after' is the proper ending to all fairy stories and romances, and we readers willingly let our imaginations stop there. But really, of course, after the 'happily ever after' comes the rest of life, just as it does after the magic of Christmas.

I don't believe it's wrong to long for the world to be different – quite the contrary. But it is disabling if that longing gets focused on one or two unreal moments that are somehow supposed to deliver perfection without any effort on our part. And part of the dissatisfaction that often sets in after Christmas is that we don't even really know what it is that we long for. We keep trying to satisfy our longing with things that we think we ought to want, and then we wonder why we're disappointed. We try to make up for it by saying, 'Well, at least the children enjoyed it', but actually we know that they are beginning to learn, too, that there is something hollow at the heart of so many of our pleasures. We try to pass on to them a formula for happiness, even though we know that it doesn't work for us, and when they begin to discover that happiness can't be bought for long with material possessions, we call it 'growing up'. We mourn the lost world of childhood illusions, because we have not discovered any other formula that works in the grown-up world.

That's why Scrooge's nephew is onto something. He is articulating what really makes Christmas a magical time – its ability to make people open up to each other and see their common humanity. This is what his sad old Uncle Scrooge has to learn. Three Christmas Spirits (and I'm sure Dickens intended the pun) come to teach Scrooge the reality of Christmas. They show him scenes from his past, his present and his future, and they help him to see how poverty-stricken his life is, for all his wealth. However rich he may be, all he has to look forward to in life is loneliness and unmourned death, unless he can discover the magical Christmas spirit of belonging that his nephew has described so eloquently.

If we come to the heart of our Christmas longings, surely this is what we will find: that we long to believe that we are loved and that we belong. That's what we are straining to say, however inarticulately, when we say that Christmas is a time for families, or that no one should be alone and hungry at Christmas. We're reaching out for a definition of what might make us really happy, because it might be what we are designed for by our maker. But we constantly seem to try to make our lives work without looking at the design, as though we can do it by ourselves. It's like trying to put together some particularly fiddly child's toy without looking at the instructions, and then wondering why it's such an odd shape and why we have those ominous-looking pieces left over.

Yet according to the gospel stories, God decides that, if we can't work out how to share our lives with each other, another plan is needed: for God to share our life. At the first Christmas, Christians believe God came, born as a human child, to show us the magic of Christmas, the magic of sharing, the magic of being what we are meant to be.

God came without any protection, with no contingency plans to be airlifted out of the human situation if it should go wrong, but simply to share our life, and to ask us to share the divine life. God requires shelter and protection and nourishment and love, just as we do, because sharing is never one way. It is never just a matter of us condescending to share out of our riches, but needing nothing in return. Part of our design is that we cannot be complete without what other people have to give us, just as they cannot be what they are meant to be without us. As the baby Jesus lies in the hay, he is demonstrating the spirit of Christmas. This is the magic – this child, come to show us that every child,

every human being, is carrying about with them the true spirit of Christmas. I believe that God gives us Jesus to share, just as God gives us every human being we meet.

We are the mad, wild magic of Christmas, every one of us. We don't have to look any further, and we will never exhaust the magical potential of other human beings. The Christmas spirit will be with us forever. We have kept looking around trying to find it in other things, when all the time it was staring us in the face, looking out through the eyes of the person next to us. It seems we keep looking for the catch – surely that can't be all there is? Surely our hearts must really desire diamonds, and not just to stretch out a hand to another human being and feel them reach out for us, too?

In his book *The Coloured Lands*, the writer G.K. Chesterton says that we often behave as though we are determined only to believe in the solemn and the unpleasant. We behave as though, now we are grown-up, we must never again believe that simple fun is the meaning of life. We constantly subvert things from their true and joyful purposes, and insist that life is prosaic and pointless. But what if, he says, some mad uncle should propose the theory that:

> *... all the objects which children use at Christmas for what we call riotous or illegitimate purposes, were originally created for those purposes; and not for the humdrum household purposes which they now serve. For instance, we will suppose that the story begins with a pillow-fight in a night nursery; and boys buffeting and bashing each other with those white and shapeless clubs. The uncle... would proceed to make himself unpopular with parents and popular with children, by proving that the pillow in prehistoric art is obviously designed to be a club; that the sham-fight in the night nursery is actually more ancient and authoritative than the whole institution of beds or bedclothes; that in some innocent morning of the world such cherubim warred on each*

other with such clouds, possibly made of white samite, mystic, wonderful, and stuffed with feathers from the angels' wings; and that it was only afterwards, when weariness fell upon the world and the young gods had grown tired of their godlike sports, that they slept with their heads upon their weapons; and so, by a gradual dislocation of the whole original purpose of the pillow, it came to be recognized as having its proper place on a bed.

Suppose we were to apply that wild principle to the whole of Christmas. I think we have hidden the truth of it from ourselves by trying to satisfy ourselves with imitations. We have tried to discover the meaning of Christmas, its spirit, its magic, in something outside itself. But, for me, the meaning is exactly what we see when we look into the cradle of the baby Jesus – it is a human life, given to be shared. If we look at our Christmas longings with the eyes of Scrooge's nephew, or of Chesterton's mad old uncle, we might be able to see their true origins. We long to love and be loved, and that is, I believe, exactly what Christmas assures us of. God loves us enough to come and share our life, not just giving out of the divine plenty, but happy to receive out of ours. In her lovely Christmas hymn, Christina Rossetti writes,

> What can I give him, poor as I am?
> If I were a shepherd, I would give a lamb.
> If I were a wise man, I would do my part,
> but what I can, I give him – give my heart.

Just as we have forgotten that, just possibly, pillows may have originally been designed for pillow fights and only incidentally for sleeping on, so we have forgotten, just possibly, that Christmas may have been designed for giving our hearts, not for trying to satisfy ourselves with other things. That, I believe, is what the baby in the manger comes to do – to ask for our hearts and to offer us his.

After his encounter with the 'Christmas spirits', Scrooge never saw them again, or needed to, because he had at last discovered the real spirit of Christmas:

> *... and it was always said of him, that he knew how to keep Christmas well, if any man alive possessed the knowledge. May that be truly said of us, and all of us! And so, as Tiny Tim observed, God Bless Us, Every One!*

CHAPTER 2

Making Lists

I know some people who start buying Christmas presents while they are on their summer holidays. While I quite admire this, I have long given up any attempts to emulate them. I don't usually give an honest reason for this, which is that I am too disorganized. Instead I give a theological reason, which is that the time leading up to Christmas is a season in its own right, and it shouldn't all be telescoped into one gigantic Christmas celebration. The four weeks before Christmas are called Advent, and they are traditionally a time of fasting and preparing ourselves for the joy of Christmas. Advent has all kinds of customs of its own, which it would be a shame to lose in the rush to get to Christmas itself. In some churches and households, the Advent wreath is the main focus of marking the time before Christmas. Every week of the four weeks of December a candle on the wreath is lit, and the great heroes of the history of our faith are commemorated, because they helped to prepare the world and us for the birth of the Christ child. Many children will have Advent calendars, with a little door for each of the days until Christmas. Behind the door there may be a picture or a biblical text or even a little square of chocolate. In my childhood we had a book that came out every Advent, and we had a chapter a night until Christmas. It was a Victorian story called *A child's Christmas*, very battered and with several pages missing, but we loved it.

It started with the making of the Christmas pudding, which was a laborious process in the days when dried fruit had to have its stones and stalks removed by hand, and bread and lemons had to be grated without any machines to help. We always made our Christmas puddings on the day we read that chapter of the book, and each member of the family was supposed to say a prayer as they stirred the pudding.

All of these customs take for granted that, mentally and imaginatively, we should walk slowly and deliberately towards Christmas, really noticing our surroundings, and not just rush into it headlong, without proper preparation.

The weeks before Christmas remind me most forcefully of pregnancy. I suppose that is partly because we know that we're waiting for the birth of a baby. But it's also because of that curious combination of readiness and unreadiness. When you are pregnant, you do everything you can to prepare for the birth of your baby, but you just cannot anticipate what the baby itself will be like. You cannot guess what it will look like or what its character will be. For that, you can only wait.

In the Christmas story, there is that same combination of knowing and not knowing what is going to happen when this baby, Jesus, is born. As Christians see things, God's preparations for the birth of Jesus make a very long and very strange list that goes back centuries. Thousands of years before Jesus is born, there are prophets who seem to be expecting God to work through the birth of a child. One of them, called Isaiah, says, 'Look, the young woman is with child and shall bear a son, and shall name him Immanuel.' 'Immanuel' means 'God is with us', and, centuries after the death of Isaiah, the followers of Jesus re-read what the prophet had written and saw it as part of God's preparations for Christmas.

Then, as we get closer to the time for Jesus to be born, God has to choose suitable parents for this wonderful baby. God's choice is a bit surprising because Mary and Joseph are very ordinary people, not rich or powerful or able to spoil the special baby with lots of possessions. The only unusual thing about Mary is that, when God sends an angel to ask her if she will be a mother to Jesus, she just says 'yes'. I don't know many people who would react so calmly to such a visit. It's intriguing to wonder if there were other women who said 'no', or who wouldn't recognize an angel if it was standing right in front of them and so didn't even notice that they were being asked. We just know that Mary said 'yes', and God's preparations got more detailed.

The person that God chooses to be a father-figure for Jesus isn't obviously outstanding either. But without him all of God's centuries of planning could have gone to waste.

The next part of God's Christmas list is to prepare the right setting for the birth. Here too God shows surprising restraint, even – dare we think it? – inefficiency. After all those centuries of making lists and getting things ready, Jesus is finally born in a stable because his parents can't find a hotel room in the crowded town. All the rest of us would book ahead, especially with everyone coming home to be counted for the census. But not God.

God does send a big group of angels, singing loudly and joyfully, but arranges all of that for a group of shepherds.

God could have sent the angels to a large and crowded city, and called all the people to come and witness the birth of Jesus and bring him presents and help to spread the good news about what God is doing. But instead all those angels set off for a hillside and sing to a small group of shepherds, and then they send them off to look at the baby. Being angels, it never enters their heads that they are perhaps over-qualified for the job God has given them. They do not think that their brightness and their music are wasted on the shepherds, because nothing that God wants can possibly be wasted.

The next group of witnesses to what God is preparing sounds more promising. Wise men come travelling the hard roads, following a star. The star must have been something very special to make the travellers set off with no other directions, just a star to follow. They must have been convinced that they were going to be in on something really big that God was preparing. After all, how long does it take to get a star ready to shine? I'm no astronomer, but I think it must probably be centuries. So, naturally, the wise men go first of all to the house of the king, a man called Herod. Where else would such an important baby be born? But King Herod, a thoroughly nasty man, has got nothing to do with God's preparations, and the wise men have to set off after their star again, until they come to the stable where Jesus lies.

Are the wise men and the shepherds baffled by God's preparations? A band of angels and a massive great star, just to call an odd assortment of witnesses to see some very ordinary parents trying to take care of a perfectly normal-looking baby? And what difference would it have made if the shepherds had refused to leave their sheep, whatever the angels said, or the wise men had stayed at home by their fires and written about the star, rather than following it? As far as we know, neither the shepherds nor the wise men played any further part in the life of Jesus, yet God seemed to want them there at the beginning.

All this planning and work on God's part and what comes of it? Just a little baby, born in obscurity, noticed only by a few strange characters. All those centuries of planning, for this? Surely there must be some mistake? Shouldn't God's action be impossible to miss? Has it all gone horribly wrong?

But perhaps, if we try to get into God's imagination, we might begin to see the point of Christmas all over again. God's strange preparations are a tender mixture of ordinary and extraordinary. Angels and stars and prophets from centuries ago join with shepherds and travellers and Mary and Joseph to celebrate God's Christmas present to us – God's Son, Jesus, who is, just as Isaiah says, Immanuel: a demonstration that God is with us.

The poet Alice Meynell captures exactly that mixture of the awesome and the normal in God's preparations when she imagines what God might be preparing for other worlds:

With this ambiguous earth
His dealings have been told us. These abide:
The signal to a maid, the human birth,
The lesson, and the young Man crucified.

But not a star of all
The innumerable host of stars has heard
How he administered this terrestrial ball.
Our race have kept their Lord's entrusted Word.

Of his earth-visiting feet
None knows the secret, cherished, perilous,
The terrible, shamefast, frightened, whispered, sweet,
Heart-shattering secret of his way with us...

Nor, in our little day,
May his devices with the heavens be guessed,
His pilgrimage to thread the Milky Way,
Or his bestowals there be manifest.

But, in the eternities,
Doubtless we shall compare together, hear
A million alien Gospels, in what guise
He trod the Pleiades, the Lyre, the Bear.

O be prepared, my soul!
To read the inconceivable, to scan
The million forms of God those stars unroll
When, in our turn, we show to them a Man.

God's preparations for Christmas didn't just begin nine months before, or even several centuries before, the birth of Jesus. God's preparations began at creation, making human beings to be like God, but we have to wait all those centuries for the penny to drop. Then we see Jesus, so like us, and we realize that actually we have to say that the other way around. Jesus is not like us, we are like him. We are born to grow more and more like Jesus and so, at Christmas time, he is born to make that possible for us. All God's preparations, from the beginning of time, have been a long list of things that would lead to this moment: the time when Jesus is born to bring us back to the truth of what we are made for.

The prophet Isaiah says:

In the wilderness prepare the way of the Lord, make straight in the desert a highway for our God. Every valley shall be lifted up, and every mountain and hill be made low; the uneven ground shall become level, and the rough places a plain. Then the glory of the Lord shall be revealed, and all people shall see it together, for the mouth of the Lord has spoken.

ISAIAH 40:3–5

So what can we do to prepare the way of the Lord? God's part is done, but Advent reminds us of our part. As we light the candles of the Advent wreath, one by one, or open each door of the Advent calendar, or shop for and cook and wrap the inessentials of Christmas, how are we getting ready to take our place in God's great plans? The baby is the clue. All of that planning, for one little baby. This is the best picture we have of the meaning of creation. All of God's creative power and might, concentrated here, ready to transform the world by sharing in it. I remember a beautiful, early evening drive through the Namib desert in southern Africa, years ago, how enchanting the light and the colours of the desert were, and how glorious the sculptures that the wind makes with the sand. But I also

remember how frightening the drive back in the dark was, because the wind and the sand had changed the landscape almost completely, and it was not at all clear where the road was any more. Making a highway through the desert's shifting sand is no easy task.

But it might be part of our Christmas preparations to imagine our lives as a great desert, full of change and uncertainty, as well as full of potential beauty. To make a highway in our lives might mean building something by which we can always find our direction. It would be strong enough and wide enough to resist the encroaching sand. It would be something that other people can use to navigate by, too. It would involve moving some things out of the way, so that the highway doesn't have to meander about in circles to reach its destination. Other things would need to be built on, so that the road doesn't fall into ditches.

The metaphor has all kinds of potential, but it requires the builders to see where they are going. Even if we cannot always see right to the end of the highway, we can see the solid road far enough ahead to be able to walk forward in trust that it is really going somewhere. Luckily, it is not something we have to engineer all by ourselves. It is a road that many people are trying to build, and parts of it are already there for us. Our job is to add our section, to encourage others to help us and to use the road that already exists. The Bible, the lives of other faithful people, the company of those who have no faith and yet long to see justice prevail – all of these are part of the Lord's highway.

But if this sounds daunting, Christmas suggests that you can start small. After all, God's planning centres around something as small as a baby.

CHAPTER 3

Decorations

Nowadays Christmas cards are the biggest part of our Christmas decorations. We get such a lot of Christmas cards, from all over the world, and they are so beautiful that we can't bear to waste them. So we cover every mantelpiece and window ledge with them, and hang them on strings across the room, and even stick them to doors and cupboards – from which they often fall with surprisingly loud and worrying plops. Actually, I quite like that, because it makes me pick up the fallen card and read it again. Some of them are pictures of classical works of art, some are photographs of the sender and their family, some are really business cards, advertising a particular institution, some are lovingly handmade. One year, a friend of ours who is a nun – and therefore has no money – made us the most beautiful, intricate star, with tiny threads pinned on card. That one is now a permanent decoration, not just for

Christmas. Some cards clearly remember that Christmas celebrates the birth of the baby Jesus, but I have noticed a growing number of cards that have reindeer or snowy scenes instead. I don't mind St Nicholas, since the original St Nicholas was doing his bit to celebrate God's great present to us, God's Son. So the story goes, he left dowries for three girls who would otherwise have had to be sold into slavery, and that seems a very good commentary on what God does at Christmas – giving us a present that helps to set us free.

There is something about Christmas that makes people feel generous, as though we have instinctively recognized something about its nature.

One of the things I love about using cards for Christmas decorations is that, both as we put them up and as we take them down, we get the chance to read them and remember the generosity of the people who sent them to us.

In cynical moments, it can seem as though Christmas decorations are just part of the increasing commercialization of Christmas. The brightly lit streets of Britain before Christmas can seem designed just to encourage people to stay out longer and shop. Although there were stars and angel-trumpeters among the Christmas lights in London this year, the main focus of the stunning display was a new animated film, which had nothing to do with Christmas at all. It was just a blatant bit of advertising, brilliantly and ingeniously occupying the night skyline. I can't help being slightly envious of the stories that a friend of mine from eastern Europe tells me about Christmas at home, which only Christians celebrate. The big public, commercial celebration comes for them at New Year.

But perhaps, even without knowing it, Christmas decorations are helping the world to rejoice in its creation. God's act in making the world, described in the Bible story of the creation in the book of Genesis, does sound quite like festive decoration. First of all there is nothing, then there is a bare and empty expanse. God begins decorating by sprinkling trees, flowers, grass, fruit trees and all kinds of vegetation liberally about. Then God hangs up the lights, which are on a very good timer switch, called day and night.

In the beginning when God created the heavens and the earth, the earth was a formless void and darkness covered the face of the deep, while a wind from God swept over the face of the waters. Then God said, 'Let there be light'; and there was light. And God saw that the light was good; and God separated the light from the darkness. God called the light Day, and the darkness he called Night. And there was evening and there was morning, the first day… Then God said, 'Let the earth put forth vegetation: plants yielding seed, and fruit trees of every kind on earth that bear fruit with the seed in it…' And God saw that it was good… And God said, 'Let the waters bring forth swarms of living creatures, and let birds fly above the earth across the dome of the sky.' So God created the great sea monsters and every living creature that moves, of every kind, with which the waters swarm, and every winged bird of every kind. And God saw that it was good… And God said, 'Let the earth bring forth living creatures of every kind: cattle and creeping things and wild animals of the earth of every kind.' And it was so… And God saw that it was good.

GENESIS 1:1–25

After that, God gets completely carried away and begins to produce living creatures, all kinds – swimming, flying, walking – all around the newly made festive scene. The most elaborately conceived shop-window Christmas display cannot begin to imitate God's imagination. Every so often God steps back and looks at creation: 'And God saw that it was good', Genesis says. God is really having fun. The whole account fizzes with divine excitement and pleasure in this process of decorating the world.

But God is a very generous artist, letting us share in creation and add our own touches. Some of them are not bad, and some of them are simply dreadful. Sometimes in our efforts to help God with the decorating we are like over-eager children, wanting to hang all the brightest lights in one clump to make a dazzling show, forgetting that that will leave other places in shabby darkness. Or we get suddenly spoiled, or over-tired, and rip all the decorations down and throw them on the floor because we cannot get them just right. Very occasionally we catch a glimpse of what God might see and add a touch that is genuinely in harmony with the divine plan. Either way, God does not surreptitiously take down what we have done and rearrange it to fit the divine vision. Instead, God lives with what we are doing and works round it, decorating over and under it, gradually finding ways to build it into the whole it is intended to be.

We may not be so generous, but that is because we are not so creative. Our temptation, when faced with so much of what we have made of the world, is to pull it all down and start again. But that demonstrates our lack of confidence. Most of the visionaries, when they talk about God's coming, can just begin to imagine how God will be able to transform the world into something recognizably the same and yet astonishingly different.

The wilderness and the dry land shall be glad, the desert shall rejoice and blossom; like the crocus it shall blossom abundantly, and rejoice with joy and singing.

ISAIAH 35:1–2

That's how the prophet Isaiah imagines the time when God recreates the world. All the words he uses to describe what he longs for are ordinary, imaginable words, but used to paint a fresh reality. And this is exactly what God does at Christmas. God takes all the materials that are already there and makes something completely new, that we could never have imagined, because we simply do not have God's creativity. Coming to save the world, God doesn't look at it with the despair that it would seem to deserve, scrumple it up and decide to start again, making a world peopled with less troublesome creatures this time. Instead, God uses the most ordinary thing imaginable, the birth of a baby, to transform everything. In an ingenious little twist, instead of being born into an already existing family, this child creates a new one. From now on, whoever is part of the family of this child is part of God's new, transformed family and God's new, vivid world. And if we still have to use the same words to describe it, and are sometimes fooled into believing that it is actually still the old world because it looks so much the same and is made out of such familiar materials, that is because we are still learning to see with God's eyes. We will get better at it if we are prepared to practise, and if we do not keep ripping up what we have done and starting again. Part of God's creativity is God's startling patience and willingness to let the work emerge gradually. Impatient people will judge it, dismiss it and walk away, but if we can summon up the patience to wait and watch, we may begin to see what God is up to.

When we put up Christmas decorations, our aim is to make the world, or at least our bit of it, look temporarily bright and cheerful and full of promise. There is often a whiff of desperation about the brightly coloured lights and the tinsel, because we know that we are only masking reality, and that it will return with a vengeance. Soon we will have to pack all the baubles away for next year and put the Christmas tree out to be recycled and resume the burden of our normal lives.

But when God does Christmas decorations, they last forever. Cunningly, God decorates the Christmas world using things that are just part of the workaday world: ordinary working people, like Joseph the carpenter, who is to be the father and protector of the new baby; or some shepherds, just getting on with their boring menial job. Nobody takes much notice of shepherds, because they have to spend so much of their time out in the fields, and they have no gossip or anything to contribute to the bustling social life they generally miss out on. I wonder if it was partly to make the shepherds feel at home that God allowed Jesus to be born in a stable? I can imagine that the shepherds wouldn't have liked to visit the new baby if he was staying in a smart hotel. But out in the stable with the animals looking on,

the shepherds look as though they belong in God's Christmas collage, with the baby wrapped up in the straw at the centre of it.

Every character in this story plays an essential part in what God is doing through the birth of the baby Jesus. You can't take one piece away without wrecking the whole, and that means that you can't value one piece more highly than the others. The shepherds are as vital as the magnificent star. And even the baby, who is the whole point of all this scene, is content to be just that – a human baby. There is no magical, mystical light around him. The walls of his house do not gleam gold. He does not speak wise words from his rough cradle, but simply coos and cries like any other baby. Because God is not trying to use all the divine special effects to change the world and make it look good for a few hours. God is patiently, creatively and joyfully doing again what God has always done, which is to make and love the world. God does not need to hide the world under a mass of bright baubles to make it acceptable. God knows just what it is, and does not want it to pretend to be anything else but what it most truly and essentially is, what it was created to be in the beginning: a place that echoes its creator's overflowing energy and creative love.

So the baby comes to change the world, not by drawing a bright veil of illusion over it, but by living in the world as it was designed to be lived in. He lives in the world as one who knows that the world is God's and that his job is to reflect God's presence and ownership. He lives in the world as a human being made in the image of God. He lives in the world with all the world's reality of hunger, danger, hatred, disease and death, as well as love, joy and creativity, and everywhere he goes, he reflects God's reality, so that life and creativity radiate out from him. Even when he is killed, death is not strong enough to hold onto him, and is forced to let go. When Jesus is raised from the dead, he shows that God's life can even transform death.

Our Christmas decorations may never quite have the power and dynamism of God's, but we can make them part of our conscious decision to live in God's world as people who can join in with the activity of its maker. We can hang up our decorations, year by year, to celebrate with joy the creation and re-creation of the world. And when we take the decorations down again and put them away for another year, we can continue to live in the world that God decorates for us, and be part of the ongoing work of creation and restoration. We know we don't have to be anything special to join in what God is doing. No one who took part in the first Christmas story was famous for anything else at all. We can look at the world, eagerly watching for God's work, appreciating what is there, and knowing that it is still in progress, and we are part of it; but knowing, too, that it is not our creation but God's. If we come to our world seeing both its freshness and its eternity, we may then begin to bring to it, day by day, the awed joy that we bring to the temporary lights and candles of Christmas.

The great seventeenth-century poet-priest John Donne wrote a Christmas sermon that captures some of what I am trying to say about the creativity of God that we celebrate at Christmas.

*He [God] brought light out of darkness, not out of a lesser light.
He can bring thy summer out of winter though thou hast no spring.
Though in the ways of fortune, or misunderstanding, or conscience,
thou hast been benighted till now, wintred and frozen, clouded and
eclipsed, damp and benumbed, smothered and stupified till now, now
God comes to thee, not as in the dawning of the day, not as in the
bud of the spring, but as the sun at noon, to banish all shadows; as
the sheaves in harvest to fill all penuries. All occasions invite his
mercies, and all times are his seasons… 'God is thy portion,' says
David. David does not speak so narrowly, so penuriously as to say,
God hath given thee thy portion, and thou must look for no more.
But 'God is thy portion', and as long as he is God he hath more to
give and as long as thou art his, thou hast more to receive.*

God, the generous artist at work, achieves things beyond our
comprehension, and yet invites our participation and pleasure,
both at Christmas and forever.

CHAPTER 4

One of my most exciting memories of Christmas as a child is of waiting for the parcel from my grandparents. We grew up in India, and my lovely grandparents back in England made it their solemn grandparently duty to find out what other little girls of our age would be keen on in England, and to get it for us. Since there were five of us, this was no light undertaking. Faithfully, year by year, they sent us first dolls, then clothes and records, as our tastes changed. We were the first children in our school to have realistic baby-dolls that could wet themselves, and later the first to hear of Cliff Richard.

Our grandparents' parcel, when it arrived, was always beautifully wrapped, which was just as well, because its neat but festive exterior was all we saw before it was whisked away by my mother and hidden until Christmas Day. She was under the impression that she hid the box well, but we always knew exactly where her oh-so-secret hiding place was each year, and I have to confess that the box was subjected to a good deal of gazing upon, and even prodding when our mother was innocently employed elsewhere. One year she had actually opened the box before Christmas – I suppose to check which present was for which child – and that year the suspense was unbearable. In the end we decided to find out what our presents were to be. It was probably the most alarming and wicked-feeling errand I have ever run and I have to tell you that the results were not happy. Although we did identify the parcel destined for each of us, and did manage to work out that we had each been given exactly the doll we longed for, our initial joy very quickly turned to dullness. We realised that we hadn't actually wanted to know in advance, and that we were really missing the sense of anticipation and longing that went with waiting for the proper time.

So it wasn't *just* the gift itself that we wanted, we discovered. It was the whole magic of Christmas, and we had spoiled it for ourselves.

When, later, I came to read Louisa M. Alcott's classic, *Little Women*, I knew from that Christmas experience that Jo was going to have to learn that Christmas is not just about getting presents. The book starts like this: ' "Christmas won't be Christmas without any presents," grumbled Jo.' Jo is one of the daughters of the formerly affluent March family, but the family has fallen on

hard times, and it looks as though their Christmas is going to be less festive than any of them would like.

Jo surely speaks for most children (and, indeed, many adults!) in the English-speaking world in assuming that presents are the main point of Christmas. Of course, that wouldn't be true in all cultures, and Jo and her sisters quickly discover that even in nineteenth-century America, where they live, there are many, many people who have never had Christmas presents, simply because they are too poor. The girls discover the joys of giving presents, as well as getting them, when they take their Christmas breakfast to a hungry family and if the presents they do finally receive are not as large as they would once have expected, still they find themselves strangely content with their humble Christmas.

But in one very important sense, I believe that Jo is right – Christmas does indeed celebrate gift-giving, because it celebrates what God gives to us: God's own self. In simple, almost banal, words, the poet John Betjeman celebrates the real gift of Christmas:

And is it true? And is it true,
This most tremendous tale of all,
Seen in a stained-glass window's hue,
A Baby in an ox's stall?
The Maker of the stars and sea
Become a Child on earth for me?

And is it true? For if it is,
No loving fingers tying strings
Around those tissued fripperies
The sweet and silly Christmas things,
Bath salts and inexpensive scent
And hideous tie so kindly meant,

No love that in a family dwells,
No carolling in frosty air,
Nor all the steeple-shaking bells
Can with this single Truth compare –
That God was Man in Palestine
And lives today in Bread and Wine.

What are we to make of this strange gift that God gives us? Is it at all what we wanted? If we imagined that God was going to give us a present, is this truthfully what we might have expected? Perhaps we may have been thinking more along the lines of the kind of gifts that the good fairies bring to Sleeping Beauty in the old fairy story. They bring the new baby things like health and beauty, and the ability to make people love her. All of those would be genuinely delightful presents to be given, and surely well within God's means? But God's gifts seem to be rather more surprising. Look, for example, at what Mary gets when an angel comes to tell her about God's gift to her.

In the sixth month the angel Gabriel was sent by
God to a town in Galilee called Nazareth, to a
virgin engaged to a man whose name was Joseph,
of the house of David. The virgin's name was Mary.
And he came to her and said, 'Greetings, favoured
one! The Lord is with you.' But she was much

perplexed by his words and pondered what sort of greeting this might be. The angel said to her, 'Do not be afraid, Mary, for you have found favour with God. And now, you will conceive in your womb and bear a son, and you will name him Jesus. He will be great, and will be called the Son of the Most High, and the Lord God will give to him the throne of his ancestor David. He will reign over the house of Jacob for ever, and of his kingdom there will be no end.' Mary said to the angel, 'How can this be, since I am a virgin?' The angel said to her, 'The Holy Spirit will come upon you, and the power of the Most High will overshadow you; therefore the child to be born will be holy; he will be called Son of God…' Then Mary said, 'Here am I, the servant of the Lord; let it be with me according to your word.' Then the angel departed from her.

LUKE 1:26–38

I wonder if Mary's heart rose a little, after the initial shock of seeing an angel at all. After all, he starts by telling her that she has been particularly chosen by God. She could be forgiven for hoping for something rather special. And, of course, she does get something rather special, but it is going to cause her quite a lot of trouble and hardship, this present of God's, as well as a lot

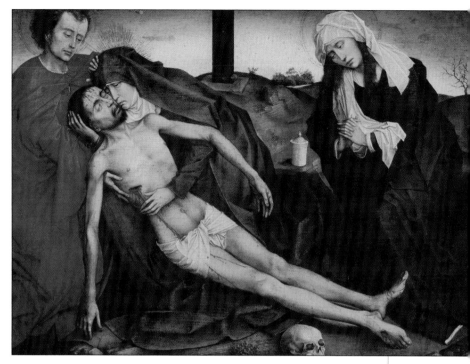

of joy. She is going to have to bring up a child whose mission will take him away from her and lead to his death. Even if she doesn't realize that to begin with, she does realize that she is going to have to face a lot of questions about the origins of her unexpected pregnancy, and it is greatly to her credit that she accepts God's unexpected present. She doesn't bargain or suggest alternatives or ask if she can swap with someone else. She simply takes what God is offering. It is going to change her life and the lives of so many others.

Mary is the ideal recipient of presents, it seems. She's the kind of person who accepts the gift with delighted curiosity and waits to see how it works. She's not the kind of person who opens their present cautiously and suspiciously, fearing the worst. Or the kind who lets it show on her face that she hates it and intends to take it back the minute the shop opens again. How lovely for God to give the best gift, the gift of Jesus, to someone who knows how to accept presents cheerfully. Any present God is going to give is likely to have unforeseen consequences, and it may not be exactly what you had asked for, but it may also change your life in ways that you couldn't imagine or begin to hope for.

George Eliot tells the story of Silas Marner, a lonely and reclusive man, who has allowed his life to become embittered and wasted after being falsely accused as a young man. He has moved away from all his former friends and is living in a village called Raveloe, where all that the neighbours know about him is that he is a miser. He comes to the point where he cannot trust himself to love anything except money. Only gold can provide the security he longs for, because it never changes. But his precious hoard of coins is stolen, and Silas is left alone and bereft. Then one night, just after Christmas, a small child, abandoned by her mother, happens to crawl into Silas's cottage, looking for warmth and shelter. The first Silas knows of this is when he sees the little girl's golden curls, gleaming in the firelight.

Gold! – his own gold – brought back to him as mysteriously as it had been taken away! He felt his heart begin to beat violently, and for a few moments he was unable to stretch out his hand and grasp the restored treasure. The heap of gold seemed to glow and get larger beneath his agitated gaze. He leaned forward at last, and stretched forth his hand; but instead of the hard coin with the familiar resisting outline, his fingers encountered soft warm curls. In utter amazement, Silas fell on his knees and bent his head low to examine the marvel: it was a sleeping child – a round, fair thing with soft yellow rings all over its head.

Silas's first thought is that, somehow, his little sister has come back to him, just as he remembered her in their childhood.

It is as though this is the last uncomplicated piece of human affection that Silas can remember, and it is interesting that he instantly associates it with the sleeping waif.

The thoughts were strange to him now, like old friendships impossible to revive; and yet he had a dreamy feeling that this child was somehow a message come to him from that far-off life: it stirred fibres that had never been moved in Raveloe — old quiverings of tenderness — old impressions of awe at the presentiment of some Power presiding over his life.

Silas is right to connect the child, Eppie, with his old life, in which he had a belief in God and people to love, because Eppie's coming is to bring him inexorably back into the circle of human relationships that he has forsaken. At first out of simple humanity, then out of duty, and then out of deep and abiding love, Silas becomes a father to Eppie, and is rewarded with her daughterly love and her loyalty. But this one relationship pulls him into a whole host of others, too, and soon Silas has friends and neighbours and a place in the community, where once he had only his gold.

What the child Eppie does for Silas Marner is what the child Jesus does for the whole world. He brings people out of their loneliness into the great family of God's people. God's Christmas gift to us may not be what we would have asked for. After all, Silas Marner thought he wanted his gold back. But instead he gets a whole new life. Instead of the things that we think we want, God gives us God's own self and all God's people, to love and cherish.

CHAPTER 5

Christmas Trees

Until a few years ago we lived in Wales, and it was always a part of our Christmas preparations to go out to the local managed forest and choose our Christmas tree. For me, the scent of pine needles is still part of the smell of anticipation. The clearing in the forest where the trees lay in piles, waiting to be taken away and decorated, was full of happy voices, pointing out the merits of particular trees or wondering if they would fit behind the sofa. It was definitely a whole-family activity, with tiny children attempting to lift up huge trees.

When the perfect tree had been chosen, we then had to take it to a wonderfully ingenious machine that tied the tree into a rough sausage-shape and wrapped it in plastic, ready for transportation. I wish someone would invent a machine like that for wrapping Christmas presents. I am someone for whom sellotape always sulks and refuses to play, so the memory of those beautifully co-operative trees in their wrappers makes me wistful.

The next stage, of course, was to get the tree back into the car so that we could take it home. This part always came as an unpleasant shock. Although we knew that we had got there in the car, and would therefore, presumably, have to return in the car, that thought always seemed to vanish without trace during the process of choosing our Christmas tree. It only dawned again when we staggered back to the car with the neatly wrapped tree, which suddenly seemed to have got much longer than – surely – it had been when we picked it out as the perfect one for us. We would look, thoughtfully, at the number of people and branches to be got into our strangely shrunken vehicle and wonder if we had made a mistake. But somehow we always managed. No one was ever left behind in favour of the tree, and we never had to go back and swap the tree for a smaller one. Children who would normally shriek in rage if forced to sit within touching distance of each other in the car would display the magic of the Christmas season, and sit squashed together with their limbs draped around the tree's strange protuberances.

Now that we live in a big city, we don't get to see our Christmas tree in its natural habitat before it arrives in our home. But we do still have the fun of decorating the tree together. I will pass over in silence, as unworthy of mention in the festive season, the intervening attempts to get the tree to stand upright and not lean drunkenly against the window, and the methods used to persuade the cat that the tree is not for her to climb, chew or use

for any other natural purposes. At the decorating stage, it is immensely useful to have people of different sizes in the family. We like our tree garish, none of this tasteful simplicity for us. We like tinsel and lights and lopsided cardboard decorations made in school years ago, though we do also have some very lovely things that kind people have sent us. They might like to know that they always get an honourable mention as we hang up their contribution to our decorations. There is one particular favourite. It is probably a St Nicholas figure, but it bears a marked resemblance to my husband, which the children find very satisfying.

Of course, Christmas trees aren't part of everyone's traditions of celebrating the season. In an essay from 1850, Dickens still thinks of the Christmas tree as a 'pretty German toy'.

The tree was planted in the middle of a great round table, and towered high above [the children's] heads. It was brilliantly lighted by a multitude of little tapers; and everywhere sparkled and glittered with bright objects. There were rosy-cheeked dolls, hiding behind the green leaves; and there were real watches (with movable hands, at least, and an endless capacity of being wound up) dangling from innumerable twigs; there were French-polished tables, chairs, bedsteads, wardrobes, eight-day clocks, and various other articles of domestic furniture (wonderfully made, in tin, at Wolverhampton), perched among the boughs, as if in preparation for some fairy housekeeping; there were jolly broad-faced little men, much more agreeable in appearance than many real men — and no wonder, for their heads took off, and showed them to be full of sugar-plums; there were fiddles and drums; there were tambourines, books, work-boxes, paint-boxes, sweetmeat-boxes, peep-show boxes, and all kinds of boxes... in short, as a pretty child before me delightedly whispered to another pretty child, her bosom friend, 'There was everything, and more.'

My computer doesn't like Dickens's description. It puts wavy green lines under it, suggesting that this sentence has gone on much too long, and that's even after I've left out half of it. But the computer hasn't got into the Christmas spirit, whereas Dickens has. He is piling up image after image, to give us the impression of the richness and generosity of the tree, as the children see it. For them, the tree contains a whole magical world, far removed from their ordinary, sensible world.

Part of the charm of the Christmas tree is exactly that power to evoke the strange and wonderful. Simply by being a tree, yet indoors, it speaks of the fact that ordinary rules do not apply during Christmas. The outside world is brought inside, or perhaps the inside world is shared with the outside – who knows which is the right description? Either way, as we deck the tree, we are celebrating a time when barriers are dissolved, when we can see magic in the ordinary.

Dickens, looking on as a grown-up, finds that the tree helps him to remember all his past Christmases, from childhood onwards. He uses the branches as a metaphor of his own growth, from one stage to the next, higher and higher up the tree, until he comes back to the present.

Now, the tree is decorated with bright merriment, and song, and dance, and cheerfulness. And they are welcome. Innocent and welcome be they ever held, beneath the branches of the Christmas Tree, which cast no gloomy shadow! But, as it sinks into the ground, I hear a whisper going through the leaves, 'This, in commemoration of the law of love and kindness, mercy and compassion. This, in remembrance of Me!'

The 'me' of whom Dickens speaks is, of course, God. The evergreen Christmas tree, which keeps its colour all through the seasons, is a reminder of the never-changing love of God, as is the blurring of the inside world and the outside world. At Christmas I believe that God, who made the whole world, comes to live in just one small part of it, as a tiny human baby. The whole, huge, mysterious 'outsideness' of God, so much more than we can imagine or domesticate, comes 'inside', into our ordinary human lives. We build our houses to keep the outside world at bay, to make safe, warm places where we can live in comfort. It is our way of managing the great world that might otherwise overwhelm us. But at Christmas we bring a tree indoors, a piece of wild nature, and we decorate it beautifully and give it a place of honour in our homes. Just for a while, we imagine a time when the inside world and the outside world live in harmony, as though it might some day be possible for us to be at home in the whole of the world, to be safe and welcome everywhere, and not to have to shut ourselves away from the world of nature.

The Bible has a vision of a time like that, too. It might not immediately remind us of Christmas trees, but it is actually very similar, as it describes domestic animals and wild animals living together, vulnerable children and malevolent snakes playing joyful games. It is, again, the idea that the world is one harmonious whole, that does not need to be divided into a safe, domestic world and a wild, outside world. Isaiah sees this as the work of God, who made the world, and who holds it together, and the Christian story of Christmas tells us that God is not content to let the world drift into separate pieces. Instead, God comes to bring things back together, to share our lives so that we can share the life of God. The prophet Isaiah describes it like this:

> **The wolf shall live with the lamb, the leopard shall lie down with the kid, the calf and the lion and the fatling together, and a little child shall lead them. The cow and the bear shall graze, their young shall lie down together, and the lion shall eat straw like the ox. The nursing child shall play over the hole of the asp, and the weaned child shall put its hand on the adder's den. They will not hurt or destroy on all my holy mountain; for the earth will be full of the knowledge of the Lord as the waters cover the sea.**

Isaiah 11:6–9

At Christmas we celebrate the joyful promise of that idea. We celebrate the possibility that the outside can come in and the two can be united. The whole Christmas story deliberately fuses the inside and the outside. The baby, who should be born inside, safe and comfortable, is born outside, in a stable. The shepherds, who normally live out in the fields, are called to go into the town and see the baby. Jesus is only born there in Bethlehem because Joseph, his father, is an insider. He belongs to the chosen people of God, the Jews, and he has to go and register his claim to belong here in Bethlehem, just as the baby is due to be born. So Jesus is born in Bethlehem because of his father's claim to be an insider. But as a result of Jesus' mission, the world has to learn that

everyone can be an 'insider' to God. There are no favourite children in God's home, and there is room in it for everyone. God, who should be outside the whole universe, holding it in being, is inside it instead, confined to just one place and time, so that all people can be 'insiders' to God, belonging in God's world.

But Christians can't help seeing the Christmas tree with eyes that know the rest of the story of Jesus. There will be another tree, for the adult Jesus, and it will carry not decorations but his human body. Jesus' preaching of a world where God comes close to us and wants us to come close to God didn't suit everybody. Then, as now, some people wanted the safe, secure world of God's love all for themselves, and felt that they could only be sure of it if other people were kept out. They needed to keep the inside world and the outside world apart, because otherwise they felt dangerously insecure. Jesus' God, who has no favourites, was not a God they wanted to hear about, and then, as now, this lead to his rejection.

So we could think of a Christmas tree as a question mark. Can we risk the exciting promise of a world where there are no insiders and no outsiders, a world where we all belong equally together? As we bring the wild tree into our homes, and cover it with beautiful decorations, we are commemorating a God who came from the glorious, divine world to share our lives, so that we can share the life of God. And that 'we' is not just a few of us: it is a promise for everyone.

CHAPTER 6

One of the great joys of Christmas for us is the music. We are fortunate enough to spend Christmas in Canterbury, to go to one of Europe's most beautiful cathedrals and listen to its wonderful choir. It's a male choir, with both adult and boys' voices, though inevitably, especially at Christmas, it's the boys who get most of the attention. It's hard to imagine how they keep going, with all the extra rehearsals and services they have to do in this season. And although some of the music they sing is well known, there is often something new to be learned as well.

By the time the choirboys come to our home for a party on Christmas Eve, with just one big service on Christmas morning to go, I would expect them to be worn out. But not a bit of it. They are still full of spirit and life, and in need of lively games to use up their spare energy.

In the seventeenth century in England, the Puritans tried to stop the celebration of Christmas. They suspected – probably quite rightly – that the population at large was intent on having a good time, and people may not have been remembering at every second of the day just what it was that they were celebrating. In particular, the Puritans were suspicious of Christmas music. Some of it was what they regarded as 'popish', with too many references to Mary and too many associations with a pre-reformation church. But also one can't help suspecting that some of the music was simply too *jolly* for the Puritans.

Music has always been acknowledged to have peculiar power to set or enhance a mood, so the Puritans had a point when they realized that they couldn't quell Christmas unless they silenced its music, too. Most cultures have stories about the magical effects of music. A Greek myth tells of Orpheus and his lyre that could play so sweetly that even the savage beasts were lulled. He was even able to play his way down into Hades in an attempt to rescue his beloved wife Eurydice.

In Welsh mythology, Queen Rhiannon has a flock of magical birds, whose singing can put the hearer into a deep trance-like sleep that can last for centuries. Shakespeare picks up the idea of

the power of music when, in *Twelfth Night*, he has Count Orsino say, 'If music be the food of love, play on.' The Count knows that certain kinds of music suit lovers and make them feel even more deeply in love. Or music can be used to invoke a sense of national pride and unity, when a national anthem is played. We are even told nowadays that it can enhance intelligence in very young children and babies. It is powerful stuff.

At the beginning of the Christmas story, particularly as it is told in Luke's Gospel, there is quite a lot of singing, and a bit of dancing too, and it always conveys a deep meaning. First of all, there is the lovely story of the meeting between Elizabeth and Mary. Elizabeth is Mary's cousin, an older woman who has given up any hope of having a baby. But an angel appears to Elizabeth's husband and tells him that they are going to have a son, a very special boy, who will play an important part in God's plan. Meanwhile, a few months later and many miles away, the same angel appears to Mary and tells her that she too is going to have a son, and that her son will be a king whose reign will never end.

Elizabeth is a respectable, middle-aged woman, and she and her husband are well known in their community as godly and reliable people. Mary, on the other hand, doesn't yet have a husband, and the Gospel writer doesn't tell us anything about her background at all. But it sounds as though she was far less supported than Elizabeth in these early months of pregnancy. Certainly, she sets off on her own, pregnant, to visit Elizabeth.

We have to guess that Mary needed to get away from the gossip and rumours that her pregnancy was causing in her own town. So she goes to stay with Elizabeth, hoping that here she will get some sympathy and help.

In those days Mary set out and went with haste to a Judean town in the hill country, where she entered the house of Zechariah and greeted Elizabeth. When Elizabeth heard Mary's greeting, the child leapt in her womb. And Elizabeth was filled with the Holy Spirit and exclaimed with a loud cry, 'Blessed are you among women, and blessed is the fruit of your womb. And why has this happened to me, that the mother of my Lord comes to me? For as soon as I heard the sound of your greeting, the child in my womb leapt for joy. And blessed is she who believed that there would be a fulfilment of what was spoken to her by the Lord.'

LUKE 1:39–45

But she gets even more than she bargained for. As soon as she steps into Elizabeth's house, the child in Elizabeth's womb starts to dance for joy. It is as though the foetus has heard God's music, singing around the baby Jesus in Mary's womb, and he just has to dance. Jesus and Elizabeth's baby, John, are to meet again as

adults, and John will again recognize Jesus, as if that womb-music has made a lasting bond between them.

Somehow, it is the simple *joy* of the child in the womb, dancing to celebrate the presence of Jesus, that is so touching. And joy is the hallmark of the next musical interlude in the Gospel, too. This time it is angels who are rejoicing. They have been sent by God to a group of shepherds sitting out on a hillside, watching their sleeping sheep. It is a perfectly ordinary night, like hundreds of others the shepherds have experienced until, suddenly, there is an angel standing in front of them in a blaze of light. Not surprisingly, the shepherds are terrified. 'But the angel said to them, "Do not be afraid; for see – I am bringing you good news of great joy for all the people. To you is born this day in the city of David a Saviour, who is the Messiah, the Lord. This will be a sign for you: you will find a child wrapped in bands of cloth and lying in a manger."' (Luke 2:10–12)

And as if that were not enough, the whole heavenly choir appears, breaking into songs of praise to God. It is as if the angels just cannot contain themselves. They have passed on the message, as instructed, to the shepherds, but they need the shepherds to feel their own amazed joy, too. Only music will really convey the totality of what they are feeling and give the shepherds some faint impression of the magnitude of what God is doing at Christmas.

John Milton spells out what the angels were singing, in their joy, to the shepherds:

Nature that heard such sound
Beneath the hollow round
Of Cynthia's seat, the airy region thrilling,
Now was almost won
To think her part was done,
And that her reign had here its last fulfilling;
She knew such harmony alone
Could hold all heaven and earth in happier union…

Such music (as 'tis said)
Before was never made,
But when of old the sons of morning sung,
While the Creator great
His constellations set,
And the well-balanced world on hinges hung,
And cast the dark foundations deep,
And bid the weltering waves their oozy channel keep…

For if such holy song
Enwrap our fancy long,
Time will run back and fetch the age of gold,
And speckled Vanity
Will sicken soon and die,
And leprous Sin will melt from earthly mould;
And Hell itself will pass away,
And leave her dolorous mansions to the peering day.

Milton is suggesting that, like the unborn baby in the womb, the whole of nature recognizes the harmony of God. Something deep in the created world reverberates to the remembered voice of God, singing it into existence. When the angels sing to the shepherds, they are singing of the creator, who is coming in Jesus to create again: to create harmony again, and put things back into their proper places in relation to each other. Jesus is coming to put things back in tune.

C.S. Lewis, too, uses the analogy of music to describe the way in which the world is made. In his children's fictional Narnia series, he describes the great Lion, who is the Christ-figure in the world of Narnia, making the world, watched by two children from our world, Polly and Diggory:

> *Polly was finding the song more and more interesting because she thought she was beginning to see the connection between the music and the things that were happening. When a line of dark firs sprang up on a ridge about a hundred yards away she felt that they were connected with a series of deep, prolonged notes which the Lion had sung a second before. And when he burst into a rapid series of lighter notes she was not surprised to see primroses suddenly appearing in every direction. Thus, with an unspeakable thrill, she felt quite certain that all the things were coming (as she said) 'out of the Lion's head'. When you listened to his song you heard the things he was making up: when you looked around you, you saw them.*

Christmas music picks up on this idea of God as composer. The world is created in joyful melody, and at Christmas joyful melody celebrates God's coming to restore the world to its proper song. It is as if, somewhere underneath all the noise and bustle and dissonance of the world we know and live in, there is a fresher, clearer world, where the angels are singing. At Christmas that original world comes closer to the surface, and we can begin to hear the singing again and feel our feet begin to join in the dance.

As the baby John whirls around in his mother's amniotic fluid, dancing for joy in the presence of Jesus, so the world dances in the presence of its creator, spinning with joy on its axis in the universe of possibilities that God has made.

Although the Christian gospel is supposed to be 'good news', it is often told in such gloomy ways by such depressed-sounding people that it is hard to hear it as the joyful thing it is. But Christmas music, joining in with the angels, helps us to catch a glimpse of God, dancing with joy at creation, filled with excited love of everything that has been made. That is the fundamental fact about human beings – we give God joy. Admittedly, we also give God grief, but the joy in us is more lasting and deeper, because it is what we are made for.

There is a strange and lovely carol that is sometimes sung at Christmas, which is all about God's 'dancing day'. I have never quite worked out what the words mean, but they give me the elated sensation of someone being whirled into a fast, exhilarating dance.

Tomorrow shall be my dancing day.
I would my true love did so chance
To see the legend of my play,
To call my true love to my dance.
Sing, O my love, O my love, my love, my love,
This have I done for my true love.

I like the idea that Christmas is God's invitation to us to join in
his dance and sing the song of creation. We may be joining in the
deep harmonies of life and helping to spread the music further
and further: the music of God's love for the world, the music of
the innate beauty of all that is, the music of the promise that God
will not abandon what has been made, but will come and dance
and sing it back into life.

CHAPTER 7

As far as I'm concerned, Christmas dinner is served on a large banana leaf, and consists of rice and several different kinds of curry, washed down with a cool, salty yogurt drink with nuts and coconut in it. It's hot, so we eat out of doors with tables arranged all round the square courtyard of the college in India where I experienced my first Christmas. That wasn't the only kind of Christmas dinner we had in India. We always got invited to the Christmas party at the Club, where the white business community gathered. They laid on a 'traditional' English Christmas dinner, with a fowl of some kind and plum pudding to follow, and someone always brought out a carefully hoarded box of chocolates, left over from their last visit 'home'. Those occasions were fun, too, but they had a definite play-acting character that made the banana-leaf feast seem much more natural. It was probably quite a good introduction to the fact that every family has its own version of Christmas food, and we all think that what we do is 'traditional'. It can be a cause of some dispute when two family traditions clash in a new marriage. It may seem trivial and not worth fighting about, what is eaten for Christmas dinner, but food is much more than just nourishment – it represents celebration and the honouring of an occasion. Most major festivals involve eating and drinking as an integral part of the enjoyment. Even in day-to-day life meals are an important punctuation of living, though not everyone would bother to mention them in giving an account of their day. It was one of the things I used to love about Enid Blyton's adventure stories. She was a very popular children's writer in my childhood, and she always described what the children had to eat. Squares of chocolate and ginger beer still evoke Blyton's whole world for me.

It's funny that food has become such a vital part of the Christmas celebration when it isn't mentioned at all in the accounts of the first Christmas. But of course, it must have been there. The shepherds sitting out in the fields in the dark must have had cheese and rough bread, maybe even lamb stew. The wise men must have brought some provisions with them for their journey, although we always imagine them as reasonably well-off and able to afford to buy local goods as they travelled. What did Mary and Joseph do for food? If the town of Bethlehem was so crowded that they couldn't even find a room for the night, despite Mary's heavily pregnant condition, presumably the food shops were also at full stretch. We know what the baby had, of course, though being very tired and hungry and stressed is not good for a mother's milk supplies, as many women all over the developing world would be able to testify.

When Jesus grew up, he was known to like dinner parties. Some of his critics pointed out his eating and drinking habits, and drew unfavourable contrasts between him and some of the more ascetic religious leaders, like John the Baptist, who is said to have lived on locusts and wild honey. Several of Jesus' stories have dinner parties as their setting, and he seems to have taught his disciples to think of the time when God will rule over all the earth as rather like a great wedding feast. We know that he didn't mind eating with disreputable people, much to the shock and disgust of some of the religious leaders of his day.

There is the story about a man called Zacchaeus, who was universally disliked because he had made his money by colluding with the occupying powers and by extorting it from his own people. Jesus chooses to stay at Zacchaeus's house, despite the rumble of disapproval from the crowd. Zacchaeus, quite rightly, sees Jesus' willingness to come and share a meal with him as a sign of acceptance and forgiveness, and he is so moved by it that he instantly decides to return all the money that he has gained by fraud.

Jesus entered Jericho and was passing through it. A man was there named Zacchaeus; he was a chief tax-collector and was rich. He was trying to see who Jesus was, but on account of the crowd he could not, because he was short in stature. So he ran ahead and climbed a sycamore tree to see him, because he was going to pass that way. When Jesus came to the place, he looked up and said to him, 'Zacchaeus, hurry and come down, for I must stay at your house today.' So he hurried down and was happy to welcome him. All who saw it began to grumble and said, 'He has gone to be the guest of one who is a sinner.' Zacchaeus stood there and said to the Lord, 'Look, half of my possessions, Lord, I will give to the poor; and if I have defrauded anyone of anything, I will pay back four times as much.'

Then Jesus said to him, 'Today salvation has come to this house, because he too is a son of Abraham. For the Son of Man came to seek out and to save the lost.'

LUKE 19:1–10

A sermon from Jesus would almost certainly not have had the same effect. But the shared meal was such a powerful symbol of trust and belonging that it broke through Zacchaeus's defences.

Jesus was clearly very much aware of the power of food, and the way in which it sets up all kinds of symbolic resonances in people. It can remind us of childhood meals, when we had no responsibilities, and when our mother prepared our favourite food. Or it can remind us of the first time we ate with the person we were beginning to fall in love with. Water is a symbol of life, because no life can be sustained without it. Naming the meaning and properties of different foods could go on for ever, some physical and some psychological, but all of them significant. On his last night on earth, knowing that he is going to die a horrible death the next day, Jesus chooses to give a dinner party for his friends. That meal has become a symbol for the Christian faith. The bread and wine that Jesus shared with his friends symbolizes God's loving, generous self-giving through Jesus' death on the cross. And, if there is pain involved in the symbol, there is also joy.

Although the wine stands for blood and the crushed grain of the bread stands for Jesus' broken body, yet wine is also for drinking in celebration and bread is also the food of life. As Jesus' followers share this food, day by day, week by week, they not only remember the past but also promise to be together as Jesus' people, sharing the family meal with each other forever. Just as Zacchaeus knows that to share a meal with Jesus is to be accepted and forgiven and changed, so do all who join in at Jesus' table.

Jesus tells his followers to go on doing this in memory of him, and to build up the community of his people; and Christians have done it ever since. Dom Gregory Dix captures this readiness to keep Jesus' commandment in the following words:

Was ever another command so obeyed? For century after century, spreading slowly to every continent and country and among every race on earth, this action has been done, in every conceivable human circumstance, for every conceivable human need from infancy and before it to extreme old age and after it, from the pinnacles of earthly greatness to the refuge of fugitives in the caves and dens of the earth. Men have found no better thing than this to do for kings at their crowning and for criminals going to the scaffold; for armies in triumph or for a bride and bridegroom in a little country church; for the proclamation of a dogma or for a good crop of wheat; for the wisdom of the Parliament of a mighty nation or for a sick old woman afraid to die; for a schoolboy sitting an examination or for Columbus setting out to discover America... for a village headman much tempted to return to

fetish because the yams had failed; …on the beach at Dunkirk; while
the hiss of scythes in the thick June grass came faintly through the
windows of the church; tremulously, by an old monk on the fiftieth
anniversary of his vows; furtively, by an exiled bishop who had hewn
timber all day in a prison camp in Murmansk; gorgeously, for the
canonisation of Saint Joan of Arc — one could fill many pages with the
reasons why men have done this, and not tell a hundredth part of them.

That's why it is perfectly proper that food should be so important
at Christmas. We do not need to separate the practical and
historical reasons for Christmas feasting from the religious and
symbolic ones. Food can do both jobs at once, quite happily. We
know that in northern countries, where Christmas also marks the
winter solstice, this was historically a good time to sit and feast
together by the fire, when there was little to do in the fields or
with the animals. We can easily eat and drink for sensible and
seasonal reasons as well as celebrating the strange generosity of
God, whose Son is born in a stable and laid in an animal's
feeding trough so that everyone will know that they are invited
to the heavenly feast.

Feeding other people is strangely satisfying. It seems to be
one of the basic human instincts to want to provide good food
for those we love. God knows this about us; indeed, it's perfectly
possible that God invented the concept. But we also know that
it's not just the food itself that matters — unless we are starving
— but the love and the care and the concern for our well-being

that the food represents. That's why the starving in our world are doubly disadvantaged; not only are they dying from lack of something that much of the world has in excess, but also they know that the rich world doesn't care about them enough to want to feed them. We in the rich world must be seeing the starving as in some way less human than our own children, for whose nourishment we go to such lengths.

Perhaps our Christmas feasting needs to learn again from the nourishment that God offers us in Jesus' body and blood. That food is for everyone, and it demands that we look to a future

when all will sit at God's table and be fed. Our own meal can never be complete while others are kept from the table.

In Dickens's wonderful story of Scrooge's conversion at Christmas, two meals mark the change in Scrooge and make us realize that he has at last discovered the value of love.

The first meal is the one that Scrooge anonymously provides for his poor clerk, Bob Cratchit, and his family. Scrooge sends them a turkey: 'It *was* a Turkey! He could never have stood upon his legs, that bird. He would have snapped 'em short off in a minute, like sticks of sealing wax.' This turkey is the beginning of Scrooge's new relationship with Bob Cratchit and his family, which is to lead, very directly, to the saving of a life. Because Scrooge is a changed man, Bob Cratchit's son, Tiny Tim, who has been very ill, gets better.

But if this meal demonstrates the flowering of generosity in Scrooge, the next one represents the realization that he too needs to receive. He had thought he needed nothing but his money, but now he knows that he needs human love too. He plucks up his courage and goes to join his nephew Fred for dinner: '"It's I. Your uncle Scrooge. I have come to dinner. Will you let me in, Fred?" Let him in! It is a mercy he didn't shake his arm off. He was at home in five minutes.'

Fred had been waiting to make his uncle at home for a very long time, but until Scrooge had learned how to make Bob Cratchit's family home a place of love, he didn't know his own need for a home. The giving and the receiving went together.

Too much of Christian teaching has suggested that we are beggars, dependent upon God's generosity. But Christmas suggests that, however much truth that teaching may contain, it is not how God sees it. God loves us and longs to feed us and nourish us. We give God pleasure by accepting God's gifts, so we can truthfully say that to receive from God is to give just what God has always wanted. We don't need to feel like a poor relation, grudgingly received in God's house. We can give and receive in that one act of letting God feed us. So Christmas food may be the best kind of celebration of God's love.

CHAPTER 8

Family

I don't remember a childhood Christmas spent only with
my immediate family. My parents very much worked on the
principle that no one should be alone at Christmas, so they
made a point of inviting anyone who looked as though they
might need it. Although we sometimes whined about this
imposition, and pointed out that our school friends only had
grannies and aunts over for Christmas dinner, and not virtual
strangers, I think we realized even then that there were
advantages to the arrangement. For one thing, the visitor nearly
always brought some kind of a present with them, and, although
I don't think we would quite have been able to put this less
tangible thing into words, they also brought us a warm glow of
virtue. I remember someone who had recently been bereaved,
someone recovering from a nervous illness and someone who
hated his own family too much to be with them even at

Christmas. We couldn't help noticing, in such company, how lucky our own lives had been. The presence of this interestingly needy stranger generally made us behave rather better, too. We would play board games and sing carols and read the bad jokes out of our Christmas crackers with a sense that our normally despised sisters were perhaps not so bad after all. I hope we weren't too patronizing to our guests who, I realize in retrospect, may sometimes have been longing to get out of our noisy and boisterous house and back to their quiet and solitude.

In my memory, this habit of sharing Christmas with a stranger just seemed so obviously a thing that a Christian family should do that I'm not sure that we ever asked our parents to justify it to us. If we had, I suspect that they would have told us part of the Christmas story. It is the part where the heavily pregnant Mary has to set off with Joseph her husband to the town where he was born, because a national census required all citizens to register in their place of origin.

In those days a decree went out from Emperor Augustus that all the world should be registered. This was the first registration and was taken while Quirinius was governor of Syria. All went to their own towns to be registered. Joseph also went from the town of Nazareth in Galilee to Judea, to the city of David called Bethlehem, because he was descended from the house and family of David. He

**went to be registered with Mary, to whom he was
engaged and who was expecting a child. While
they were there, the time came for her to deliver
her child. And she gave birth to her firstborn son
and wrapped him in bands of cloth, and laid him
in a manger, because there was no place for them
in the inn.**

Luke 2:1–7

The traditional Christmas nativity play adds all kinds of details to
this story. I always have to remind myself, for example, that the
donkey who carries Mary is a fictional addition, and that the
actual story doesn't tell us how Mary and Joseph travelled.

Nor does it show us the increasingly frantic efforts of Joseph
to find somewhere for Mary to go into labour. School and
church nativity plays generally have at least two innkeepers who
turn Joseph and Mary away peremptorily before we get to the
third rough but kind innkeeper, who suggests his stable as a last
resort. This has the advantage of providing parts for several
children, but it is just as likely, if you read the story, that the
baby was born out in the fields, and laid in an outdoor feeding
trough. After all, many babies are born under such conditions,
all over the world.

But the heart of the story remains the same – that Jesus is
born in conditions of homelessness and discomfort, and his first

resting-place is a makeshift cradle, none too clean, borrowed in desperation. The irony of this is quite clear to the Gospel writers – this is the Son of God, through whom the heavens and the earth are made, and yet he doesn't even have anywhere to be born.

The poet and writer G.K. Chesterton brings this out clearly in one of his poems:

> There fared a mother driven forth
> Out of an inn to roam;
> In the place where she was homeless
> All men are at home.
> The crazy stable close at hand,
> With shaking timber and shifting sand,
> Grew a stronger thing to abide and stand
> Than the square stones of Rome.
>
> For men are homesick in their homes,
> And strangers under the sun,
> And they lay their heads in a foreign land
> Whenever the day is done…
>
> To an open house in the evening
> Home shall all men come.
> To an older place than Eden
> And a taller town than Rome.

To the end of the way of the wandering star,
To the things that cannot be and that are,
To the place where God was homeless
And all men are at home.

What Chesterton is suggesting is that God comes, born as a homeless
child, so that we can have a home. We carry with us always a sense

of not quite belonging, what Chesterton calls 'homesickness'. Most of the time this is buried, and when it does surface, we are hard put to it to say what it is that we long for; but Chesterton, a practising Christian, is convinced that it is the longing for our real home in God. We have strayed so far from home that we have forgotten even that *that* is what we yearn for, and that is why Jesus comes to show us our homelessness and take us home with him.

Those of us who live in comfort and reasonable security may find it harder to admit that we are actually homesick. We may well experience times of sadness and emptiness, and a sense of meaninglessness, as though we belong nowhere and no one cares for us, and nothing we do is worthwhile; but we may very well not know the source of these feelings. Chesterton would argue that they come from a profound dislocation of our whole being, as though we were snatched from home in infancy and have been homeless ever since. But the memory of our true home is so distant that we can hardly bring it to the surface at all. So what God does at Christmas is to do a kind of play for us. God leaves home in heaven and comes to be born as a human child, but not into a warm, safe home, but out in the fields, or in a barn. 'Look', God says, 'this is the human condition. This is how life is for all of you.' And then God says, 'But I have come to take you home. I have come to share your homelessness so that you can come home with me.'

All through his earthly life Jesus, God living with us, has no fixed home. He says of himself, 'Foxes have holes and birds of the air have their nests, but the Son of Man has nowhere on earth to lay his head.' (Matthew 8:20) It is as though this is the only way in which he can keep before his own mind and ours that God is the only true home-maker.

For most of the time, many of us can mask our homesickness. Our comfort and our possessions and our food and our warmth can convince us that we are all right. That's why Jesus often said that it is harder for rich people to know that they need God. We have so many things that we hardly recognize the neediness in ourselves.

Our world is very full of people who are genuinely homeless and in need. In the midst of  Western affluence there is striking poverty, even if we are not prepared to see it. And in some countries, whole communities live with a level of destitution that we would find unbearable. At Christmas, charities spring into action to try to provide food and shelter and company for homeless people, even if only for a short time. For some of the people who come to Christmas shelters, this will be their annual conversation. Most of the year they have to put up with transactional contact only, between them and social services, or passers-by or the police; but at Christmas they can remember what it is like to be part of human society and treated with respect, as though they might have interesting views of their own and contributions to make to society. At Christmas these charities and their volunteers are responding, whether they would put it like this or not, to the Christian story of a homeless God.

God, the power who made all things and keeps them all in being, chooses this way to come and live with us; so perhaps we might see this as a vision statement setting out for us what God's priorities are. God, it seems, is not much interested in security or safety or comfort or status or wealth. The people God calls to be parents to Jesus and to witness his birth are not important or influential. He comes as a baby, utterly at the mercy of the people around him, as all babies are. And, just like all children, some people respond with love and care to his vulnerability, and protect and nurture him, while others are only interested in their own needs. Hard as it is to imagine, if Mary and Joseph had been neglectful or abusive parents, they would have had it in their power to hurt or kill the Son of God, just as so many other human children are killed by those who should be protecting them.

It is as though God is trying to suggest to us a way of defining again what it is to be human. It is not a new definition, because it is one that we instinctively recognize as we try to feed hungry and homeless people at Christmas. Deep in our hearts, we know that human beings are not best described in terms of what they do or own. Human beings carry with them, wherever they go, and however much they may have degraded it in some way or another, their original likeness to God. The creation story of the Jewish scriptures tells us that we are 'made in God's image', and that is what the baby Jesus comes to remind us of. We are like

God because we are capable of loving unselfishly. The true human image is not a king or a soldier or a popstar or a millionaire, but a baby. And the true human community is one that will do its utmost to protect the vulnerable and the needy, as Mary and Joseph do for the baby Jesus. They don't know he is God, they just know that he needs them, and they respond. Not all communities or families are like that, as we know to our sorrow. But where we do encounter such attitudes, we know we are home, and where we can respond ourselves, as Mary and Joseph do, we know we can make a home for others.

CHAPTER 9

Christmas Eve

My two favourite memories of Christmas Eve services couldn't be more different. One comes from a time when we lived in the country and went out to a tiny village church where my father was to conduct the service. There were very few people there because the village was very small, and most of the housing was now a long way from the church. It was also bitterly cold inside the little church, which wasn't used very often. To begin with, it felt like a bit of a waste of time being there at all. We had driven quite a long way, down very narrow winding roads, and would have to drive back again after sharing Midnight Mass with half a dozen people. But gradually, as the service progressed, there was a great sense of joy and intimacy, as though the stones of the church were giving back the voices and feelings of all the thousands of people who had worshipped God there over the centuries.

When we came out of church into the quiet, dark countryside, we felt as though we really had heard the angels calling us to come and see the baby Jesus.

My second memory is of a midnight service in a bustling seaside town, where my husband grew up. We were there for Christmas, and he was helping with the service in the church where he had been a choirboy. Like many churches on Christmas Eve it was very full, and a lot of the congregation were not terribly familiar with church services. Some were rather merry, having spent most of the earlier part of the evening in the local pub. But there was still a very strong sense in the town that the proper thing to do on Christmas Eve is to go to Midnight Mass. I am amazed and delighted at the way this custom persists, even among people who have very little time for churchgoing during the rest of the year. It is as though the birth of the baby Jesus breaks through to the real heart of people's religious sensibilities in a way that ordinary churchgoing often doesn't.

On this particular Christmas Eve, we soon became aware of a very young and very drunk couple who had come to church in considerable distress. The girl in particular started to weep during the first hymn and seemed unable to stop. They stayed on at the end of the service and talked and talked. They had come to church almost without thinking about it, and then something about the service had crept under their guard. For the girl, it seemed to be something about the baby in the manger, in his need and vulnerability. The boy seemed to feel that he should be protecting and helping the girl in her distress, but he was baffled by inexperience and inebriation. When at last they went home, they were vowing to put their relationship on a proper footing and stand by each other. I have no idea if that promise survived the terrible headaches they would both have the next day. But they had shown how touching the Christmas story is.

It is strange that it is not the thought of the power of God that moves people, but the vulnerability of God. It is the baby lying in the straw that we sing and praise at Christmas. The mysterious, majestic power of God that makes this birth possible is somehow very much in the background as we concentrate on the fragility of the human child. The world is very used to power. Many of us long for it, many more have been hurt by it. We have learned to distrust power, even though we would rather have it than not. But we do believe that power corrupts and absolute power corrupts absolutely. Indeed, that is probably one of the most widely accepted of maxims. Whether they like to admit it or not, the Christian churches have considerable power and influence, and they have not been afraid to use it over the past two millennia. Only very occasionally, for example in the formation of the Franciscan movement, have the churches been willing to risk imitating God's way in the world as Jesus shows it at Christmas. The ruler of the universe, the source of all life, comes to redeem his people not by force, not even by overwhelming them with the sight of the divine majesty, but as a little child.

In a profound meditation on this contrast between worldly power and the activity of God, the twentieth-century theologian Austin Farrer writes:

> Yet Mary holds her finger out, and a divine hand closes on it. The maker of the world is born a begging child; he begs for milk, and does not know that it is milk for which he begs. We will not lift our hands to pull the love of God down to us, but he lifts his hands to pull human compassion down upon his cradle. So the weakness of God

proves stronger than men, and the folly of God proves wiser than men.
Love is the strongest instrument of omnipotence, for accomplishing
those tasks he cares most dearly to perform; and this is how he brings
his love to bear on human pride; by weakness not by strength, by need
and not by bounty.

It is as though God sees to the very heart of our being and sees
that it is good. He does not show us our sinfulness and our need,
but our kindness and our compassion. He brings out the best in
us. The child in the manger needs us and we respond.

When you read the gospel accounts of Christmas, it is
extraordinary to notice how little the baby himself is mentioned.
We are not told what he looked like or whether he was a
particularly good baby. Did he feed well? Did he sleep well? How
did he react to his odd visitors? What colour were his eyes? We
know none of those things. He was just a baby. We know how
God prepared Mary and Joseph for the birth, and how shepherds
and wise men were summoned to witness it, but the central
moment of Christmas Eve is over in one sentence in Luke's
Gospel, 'And she gave birth to her firstborn son and wrapped
him in bands of cloth, and laid him in a manger, because there
was no place for them in the inn.' It is a surprisingly abrupt
announcement of the birth of the world's saviour.

Anyone who has ever been through or witnessed childbirth
will have some idea of the pain and strain that is encapsulated in
that one sentence. Most of us in the modern Western world

don't like to imagine what it would be like to give birth in such conditions, with no pain-controlling measures and no medical back-up, though that is still the way in which many of our sisters in the rest of the world have to experience childbirth. Most of us would not like to have to travel far on rough roads nearing the end of pregnancy, as Mary did. She and Joseph had had to travel from Nazareth to Bethlehem, on packed roads, at the whim of an Emperor who had decided to call for a census. Joseph had to go back to the town where he was born to register, and he had to take a very pregnant Mary with him. We don't know how they travelled, but it's hard to believe that it could have been comfortable. As she packed her bag for the journey, Mary must also have included the essentials, in case the baby was born along the way. Certainly, when the time comes, she has the bands of cloth to wrap him in, all ready and waiting. But that's about all the comfort she does have. Although Joseph was born in Bethlehem, he doesn't seem to have had any family left there, because he and Mary have nowhere to stay in a town plunged into chaos by the census arrangements.

All of this we can imagine behind the bald sentence announcing Jesus' birth. Imagining the details of Jesus' birth has been a popular pastime for much of Christian history.

The mystery plays that were performed in the Middle Ages, for example, import all kinds of extra characters, like a midwife to help Mary with the birth. But the Gospel writers just stick to the bare bones of the story. They want us to get a sense of what is

happening here, of the contrast between the magnitude of what God is doing and the very ordinary methods used to accomplish it.

It is John's Gospel that really brings out the meaning that the others hint at. Like Luke, John hardly mentions the birth of the child, but he leaves us in no doubt about what is going on.

In the beginning was the Word, and the Word was with God, and the Word was God. He was in the beginning with God. All things came into being through him, and without him not one thing came into being. What has come into being in him was life, and the life was the light of all people. The light shines in the darkness, and the darkness did not overcome it… And the Word became flesh and lived among us, and we have seen his glory, the glory as of a father's only son, full of grace and truth.

JOHN 1:1–5, 14

The birth is summed up in one phrase: 'the Word became flesh' – a human being. John wants us to picture the Word, living in power with God the Father, creating the world, the source of all its life. *This* is what becomes flesh. The extraordinary power that enabled the whole universe is suddenly contained in a human baby. John wants us to feel the shock of that, to make

our imaginations reel as we try to think of what that means.

But if John starts with the big picture – the creative life of God – Christians believe that at Christmas God starts with the small picture. A child is something we can understand. A human baby is a symbol of life and hope. Each new human life is miraculous. A whole new person comes into existence.

This little commonplace miracle of birth is something that we almost take for granted. But in the birth of the baby Jesus, this is what God is offering over and over again. This is an integral part of the nature of God, to make new life. That is why there is any life at all, because the creator of the universe is so full of life that it pours out into the world. God is always life-giving, and the birth of Jesus is God's offer of new life. A baby starts the world with a clean slate. It can discover its own character. It can interact with what is around it and experience and change and grow. In Jesus, God offers us the chance to start a new life, as though we were born again as babies. We can be born into the family of God and learn from that family environment. Life is natural to God, who does not begrudge it to us or force it on us. But as we look at the baby Jesus with love and compassion, God hopes we might see that we are longing to be always what we are in that moment. Just like the few people at Midnight Mass in the quiet country church, or the weeping girl by the seaside, as we look at the baby we are touched. We long to feel that we might change into the kind of people who could always sense the presence of the angels and respond with love and kindness to the world around us. And at Christmas, God says, 'Nothing is impossible.'

CHAPTER 10

Epiphany

When our children were very small, an aunt knitted them a nativity scene, complete with Holy Family, shepherds, sheep, cattle and wise men bearing gifts. It was a work of art, and it still comes out every Christmas. As it was knitted, it could safely be played with by little hands and was easily mended if any accidents befell it. A neighbour's dog came visiting one year and was much taken with one of the wise men; although the present he is carrying is now an odd sort of shape, there were no other lasting ill effects. At the start of December every year, the wise men begin their journey from some distance away from the stable, and the little knitted baby is kept somewhere safe until after the service on Christmas Eve.

The temptation, of course, is to allow the wise men to arrive in time to witness the birth of the baby. Most cribs that you see do have the shepherds and the wise men together in adoration.

But in fact, the wise men should only arrive after the shepherds are long gone to feed their hungry sheep, and just before all the Christmas decorations come down. The wise men are the last on the scene. They have come a long way, and they have taken one or two wrong turns, but they make it in the end.

In the time of King Herod, after Jesus was born in Bethlehem of Judea, wise men from the East came to Jerusalem, asking, 'Where is the child who has been born King of the Jews? For we observed his star at its rising, and have come to pay him homage.' When King Herod heard this, he was frightened, and all Jerusalem with him; and calling together all the chief priests and scribes of the people, he inquired of them where the Messiah was to be born. They told him, 'In Bethlehem of Judea; for so it has been written by the prophet: "And you, Bethlehem, in the land of Judah, are by no means least among the rulers of Judah; for from you shall come a ruler who is to shepherd my people Israel."' Then Herod secretly called for the wise men and learned from them the exact time when the star had appeared. Then he sent them to Bethlehem, saying, 'Go and search diligently for the child; and when you have found him, bring me word so that I may also go and pay him homage.' When they had heard the king, they set out; and there, ahead of them, went the star that they had seen at its rising, until it stopped over the place where the child was. When they saw that the star had stopped, they were overwhelmed with joy. On entering the house, they saw the child with Mary his mother; and they knelt down and paid him homage. Then, opening their treasure chests, they offered him gifts of gold, frankincense, and myrrh. And having been warned in a dream not to return to Herod, they left for their own country by another road.

MATTHEW 2:1–12

Notice the mistakes that the wise men make in their search for
the baby Jesus. First of all, they assume that only a king could be
important enough to have a star to mark his birth; so when they
get close they give up following the star and head for the court
instead. Next, although they have trusted the guiding star for a
great distance, now they suddenly decide that they can manage
without it, so certain are they of where it must be heading. The
star waits patiently, and as soon as the wise men leave Herod's
court, there it is, ready to guide them to their true destination.
And finally, they trust King Herod and set off to find the baby king
for him. They are clearly people with a great deal of respect for
the ruling monarchy and for proper authority, and I imagine they
expect to do rather well out of being the first to acknowledge the
new power in the land.

But they are clearly rather naïve, for all their cleverness. Herod
has only one thought in his head, and that is to hang on to power
at all costs. As soon as he hears of the new king, he plans to kill
him. Poor, wicked Herod. This is obviously the moment he has
been dreading all his life. It is almost as though, in his heart of
hearts, he has always known that he does not deserve to be king,
and that someone better will come and wrest the throne away
from him. He never for one moment questions the wise men's
assumption that the star must be proclaiming a new king.

It seems that Herod's advisers, the chief priests and legal
experts, have also had their doubts about the legitimacy of
Herod's rule. They are not at all surprised when they are

summoned to tell him what was prophesied about the great king who is to come. It is as if they have been doing their own research, privately, and have just been waiting for the moment when it would be needed. It is not often that you get the chance to frighten the living daylights out of a king, and his advisers make no effort to soften the blow. Perhaps they are enjoying themselves.

Secretly, Herod makes a pact with the innocent wise men. They are to find the baby and report back. If they really believe that Herod will go and kneel before the new king and abdicate in his favour, then they must be even less worldly than they seem.

The wise men step out of the intrigue and the music and the snide laughter and the flaring torches of the court, back into the clear, white light of the star that they have followed for so long.

It is as clear as it has been throughout their journey, and it stops with perfect certainty over one house. There is no mistaking its intentions. And now the wise men redeem themselves. For all their foolishness up until now, when they see the baby they are 'overwhelmed with joy'. He is not at all what they were expecting. He is clearly not a king, but a perfectly ordinary baby in a simple house with a peasant mother. But the wise men see, at last, as though the light from the star has finally illuminated their inner being: they see that here is the end of their quest, and it is glorious.

The presents they choose for the baby make it clear how much they have learned. They open their treasure chests and ponder, and choose gifts that are just right for this special child. Perhaps they had intended to pour out all the contents of the chest in front of the new king, to impress him with their wealth and status and to buy his favour. But now they know that such behaviour is inappropriate for the child they have found. Instead, they select just three gifts, and they are perfect. They choose gold, because they do know that, even if this baby is not a king as Herod is, yet he is kingly beyond anything they have ever met before. Then they choose frankincense, the spice that can be burnt on the altar of God. They know that they are in God's presence, as they kneel in front of the baby. And lastly, poignantly, they choose the burial

herb, myrrh. If they have been puzzled by the combination of humility and glory that their star has led them to, they realize that others will be horrified and angry. Like Herod, many will react to Jesus with violence, hating his challenge to their accepted notions of power. They will try to kill him, and they will even imagine that they have succeeded.

When they have given their uniquely insightful presents, and demonstrated how much they have learned, at last, the wise men

go home. They do not report back to Herod, and we never hear of them again.

Perhaps before they met the baby, the wise men had imagined that they would stay at the court of the new king, in honoured positions, pointed out to all who came as the clever people who first divined the birth of the great king. But now that they are genuinely wise, as opposed to just clever, they know that they have done what they came for and they are satisfied.

There is something about the wise men that catches the imagination. Although we know so little about them, somehow we identify with them. We do not know where they came from, or what they did for a living, or when they first saw the star, or with what instruments. We don't even know how many of them there were. Traditionally, we assume that there are three of them because they give three gifts, but the story doesn't actually say so. The wise men get there under their own steam and by their own cleverness. They know how to watch the heavens, and they know that the star they see is unusual and hugely significant. They know how to set about a long journey, and they have enough self-confidence to call on kings. They have good reason to think well of themselves, and they are both nearly right and profoundly wrong. But if when they set out they are only quite wise men, their wisdom is still enough to recognize the greatness of what they see and worship it.

In a touching meditation, Evelyn Waugh talks to the wise men as those who represent all of us who trust in our human wisdom alone.

How laboriously you came, taking sights and calculating, where the shepherds had run barefoot! How odd you looked on the road, attended by what outlandish liveries, laden with such preposterous gifts!... Yet you came, and were not turned away. You too found room before the manger. Your gifts were not needed, but they were accepted and put carefully by, for they were brought with love. In that new order of charity that had just come to life, there was room for you, too. You were not lower in the eyes of the holy family than the ox or the ass. You are... patrons of all latecomers, of all who have a tedious journey to make to the truth, of all who are confused with knowledge and speculation, of all who through politeness make themselves partners in guilt, of all who stand in danger by reason of their talents.

At the crib of Jesus all are welcome, and that is what the wise men tell us. Over the centuries, they have come increasingly to represent everybody. Artists begin to paint the wise men to represent different races – Western, Arab and black. They portray them as men at different stages of their lives – a youth, a man in his prime and an old man. They are all of us, called from all over the world to witness the birth of the new, strange king and be changed by it. Jesus' God is not just the possession of people who already know him or of people who are already pure in heart. He draws around the cradle of his new kingdom all kinds of people with all kinds of talents. The only thing they all have in common is that when they see the baby, they know that they have seen someone who will change their lives. Perhaps the wise men and the shepherds spent the rest of their lives telling the story of this great event. Perhaps every time they told it they saw more and more how all of their lives had prepared them to recognize the baby when they saw him. But the wise men in particular are there to tell us that the same will be true of all of us. Whatever our lives have been up until now, as we look at the baby lying in the straw we can see in him the loving activity of God. We can look back over the whole of our lives and know that everything, even the things that we are most ashamed of, even the things we know to have been wrong, have been preparing us to see this baby and know him and accept his gift of life.

Text Acknowledgments

pp. 8–9,11–12, 33, 40, 43, 55–56, 68, 76, 78, 88–89, 97–98, 102, 113, 117–118 Scripture quotations are from the New Revised Standard Version published by HarperCollins Publishers, copyright © 1989 by the Division of Christian Education of the National Council of the Churches of Christ in the USA, and are used by permission. All rights reserved.

p. 53 'Christmas' by John Betjeman, reproduced by permission of John Murray Publishers

p. 99 'Christmas Poem' by G.K. Chesterton, reprinted by permission of A P Watt Ltd on behalf of The Royal Literary Fund

Picture Acknowledgments

p. 13 Journey to Bethlehem and the Magi before Herod. Como, Church of Sant'Abbondio © 1990, Photo Scala, Florence.

p. 14 Tintoretto (1518–1594): Flight into Egypt – detail (Holy Family). Venice, Scuola Grande di San Rocco © 1990, Photo Scala, Florence.

p. 17 Illustrated London News Picture Library

p. 20 Honthorst, Gerrit van (1590–1656): Adoration of the Child. Florence, Galleria degli Uffizi © 1990, Photo Scala, Florence – courtesy of the Ministero Beni e Att. Culturali.

p. 25 E.J. Walker/Illustrated London News Picture Library

p. 28 Gaddi, Taddeo (c. 1300–1366): Annunciation to the Shepherds. Florence, Santa Croce © 1990, Photo Scala, Florence/Fondo Edifici di Culto – Min. dell'Interno.

p. 32 The Path of the Sun through the stars on the night of the 4th July 1442, detail of Taurus, from the soffit above the altar, Pesello, Giuliano d'Arrighi / Old Sacristy, San Lorenzo, Florence, Italy, Alinari / Bridgeman Art Library

p. 34 Guillaumet, Gustave (1840–1887): The Sahara. Paris, Musee d'Orsay © 1998, Photo Scala, Florence.

p. 38 Gozzoli, Benozzo (1420–1497): Saint Nicholas of Bari. San Gimignano, Sant'Agostino © 1992, Photo Scala, Florence – courtesy of the Ministero Beni e Att. Culturali.

p. 41 Zucchi, Jacopo (1541– c. 1589): Allegory of Creation. Rome, Galleria Borghese © 1990, Photo Scala, Florence – courtesy of the Ministero Beni e Att. Culturali.

p. 45 Barocci, Federico (1526–1612): Nativity. Madrid, Prado © 1996, Photo Scala, Florence.

p. 48 Millet, Jean Francois (1814–1875): The Gleaners. Paris, Musee d'Orsay © 1990, Photo Scala, Florence.

p. 55 Angelico, Fra (1387–1455): Annunciation. Florence, Museo di San Marco © 1990, Photo Scala, Florence – courtesy of the Ministero Beni e Att. Culturali.

p. 57 Weyden, Roger van der (c. 1399–1464): Pieta'. Brussels, Musees Royaux des Beaux-Arts © 1990, Photo Scala, Florence.

p. 59 The Child in a White Shirt Reading, Renoir, Pierre Auguste / Private Collection / Bridgeman Art Library

p. 63 Welliver, Neil (b. 1929): Shadow, 1977. New York, Museum of Modern Art (MoMA) © 2005, Digital image, The Museum of Modern Art, New York/Scala, Florence. Oil on canvas, 8' x 8' (243.8 x 243.8 cm). Gift of Katherine Lustman-Findling, Jeffrey Lustman, Susan Lustman Katz, and William Ritman in memory of Dr. Seymour Lustman. 992.19

p. 69 The Peaceable Kingdom, Hicks, Edward / © Worcester Art Museum, Massachusetts, USA / Bridgeman Art Library

p. 71 Rubens, Peter Paul (1577–1640): Christ on the Cross. Munich, Alte Pinakothek © 1990, Photo Scala, Florence.

p. 73 Choirboys Procession, Cooke, Stanley / Private Collection / Bridgeman Art Library

p. 74 Bruegel, Jan the Elder (school): Orpheus. Rome, Galleria Borghese © 1990, Photo Scala, Florence – courtesy of the Ministero Beni e Att. Culturali.

p. 77 Albertinelli, Mariotto (1474–1515): Meeting of Mary and Saint

Elizabeth. Florence, Galleria degli Uffizi © 1996, Photo Scala, Florence – courtesy of the Ministero Beni e Att. Culturali.

pp. 82–83 Ferrari, Gaudenzio (c. 1475–1546): Angels Playing Music. Saronno, Sanctuary © 1990, Photo Scala, Florence.

p. 86 Foppa, Vincenzo (c. 1425– c. 1515): Madonna della Tenda (Madonna of the Drape). Florence, Private Coll. © 1990, Photo Scala, Florence.

p. 87 David, Gerard (c. 1450–1523): Marriage at Cana. Paris, Louvre © 1990, Photo Scala, Florence.

pp. 90–91 Titian (1477/89–1576): Last Supper. El Escorial, Monastery of San Lorenzo © 1990, Photo Scala, Florence.

p. 93 Bruegel, Pieter the Younger (1564– c. 1637): Wedding Banquet. Ghent, Museum voor Schone Kunsten © 1990, Photo Scala, Florence.

pp. 100–101 Gentile da Fabriano (c. 1370–1427): Adoration of the Magi: panel of the predella with the Nativity. Florence, Galleria degli Uffizi © 1990, Photo Scala, Florence – courtesy of the Ministero Beni e Att. Culturali.

p. 103 Illustrated London News Picture Library

p. 107 Munch, Edvard (1863–1944): The Old Church of Aker. Oslo, Munch Museum © 1990, Photo Scala, Florence.

p. 112 The Beginnings of the Christmas Play, cover of The Illustrated London News, 1935, Broderick, Muriel / The Illustrated London News Picture Library / Bridgeman Art Library

p. 114 Chierici, Gaetano (1838–1920): First Steps. Genoa, Galleria d'Arte Moderna © 1990, Photo Scala, Florence.

p. 117 Robbia, Luca della, the Younger (1475–1550): Creche. Caldine, Convent of Santa Maria Maddalena © 1992, Photo Scala, Florence.

p. 121 The Three Kings. Ravenna, Church of Sant' Apollinare Nuovo © 1990, Photo Scala, Florence – courtesy of the Ministero Beni e Att. Culturali.

p. 122 Mowbray, Harry Siddons: The Magi. ca. 1915. Washington DC, Smithsonian American Art Museum, Washington DC © 2001, Photo Smithsonian American Art Museum/Art Resource/Scala, Florence.